PURCELL

# Te Deum Laudamus

IN D · FOR ST CECILIA'S DAY, 1694

for 2 soprano, 2 alto, tenor & bass soli,
SSATB & instruments

*edited by J. F. Bridge. Latin arrangement*
*by R. R. Terry*

Order No: NOV 070247

**NOVELLO PUBLISHING LIMITED**
8/9 Frith Street, London W1V 5TZ

# PREFACE

Although adaptations are generally open to question on artistic grounds, the practical object of this particular one carries its own justification. The authorised Latin text of the Ambrosian Hymn is *de rigeur* whenever it is used liturgically in the Catholic Church. Most available musical settings (save the Plainsong) are either beyond the capacity of average choirs, or are too baldly simple and trivial to merit serious attention. In Purcell's work, beauty, breadth, and dignity are combined with technical simplicity in so marked a degree that any ordinary choir could satisfactorily perform the music.

In preparing this edition it was necessary that the order of the authorised Latin text should be preserved, without doing violence to Purcell's music. *Time values* only of notes have sometimes been altered to fit the quantities of the Latin syllables, but nothing written by Purcell has otherwise been changed. As an illustration of the Editor's anxiety to leave Purcell untouched, he may point to the alto solo on p. 24, where he has allowed the penultimate syllable of " speravimus " to fall on an accented note (rather than alter the two characteristic minims in bars 6 and 12), when it would have been easy to write—

On p. 2, line 2, "Omnis," and on p. 22, line 3, " Domine," have been interpolated to meet the exigencies of the music, but as these words also appear elsewhere in their correct places in the text, the decrees of the " Sacred Congregation of Rites " are observed. As regards the musical text, Sir Frederick Bridge's Bi-Centenary Edition has been followed throughout.

R. R. TERRY.

*May,* 1902.

# TE DEUM LAUDAMUS
## IN D.

PRELUDE.
*Maestoso.* ♩ = 96.

Henry Purcell.

2

11415

4

ti - bi___ cœ - - li, om - nes An - ge - li et

ti - bi cœ - - li, om - nes An - ge - li et u - ni-ver-sæ

An - ge - - li om-nes An - ge - li et u - ni-ver-sæ

**Soprano I.**     **D** *mf*

u - ni-ver-sæ po - tes - ta - - tes. Ti - bi Che-ru-bim et Se - ra-

**Soprano II.**     *mf*

Ti - bi Che-ru - bim___ et___ Se - ra-

**Alto.**

po - - tes - ta - - tes.

po - - tes - ta - - tes.

**D**

*mf*

*attacca*

*May be sung by all the Altos.   **May be sung by all the Tenors.

8

-ta-rum lau - - da - - - - - - - - -

- - - bilis nu-me-rus. Te Mar - - ty-

Bass.*
SOLO.

_f_   _p_

-rum can-di-da - - - tus lau - - dat ex - er - - ci-tus.

CHORUS.
Soprano.

_ff_ Te per or-bem ter - ra-rum sanc-ta con-fi - te-tur Ec-cle - - si - a,

Alto.

_ff_ Te per or-bem ter - ra-rum sanc-ta con-fi - te-tur Ec-cle - - si - a,

Tenor.

_ff_ Te per or-bem ter - ra-rum sanc-ta con-fi - te-tur Ec-cle - si - - a,

Bass.

_ff_ Te per or-bem ter - ra-rum sanc-ta con-fi - te-tur Ec-cle - si - a,

_ff_ Tutti

*May be sung by all the Basses.

11415

_attacca_

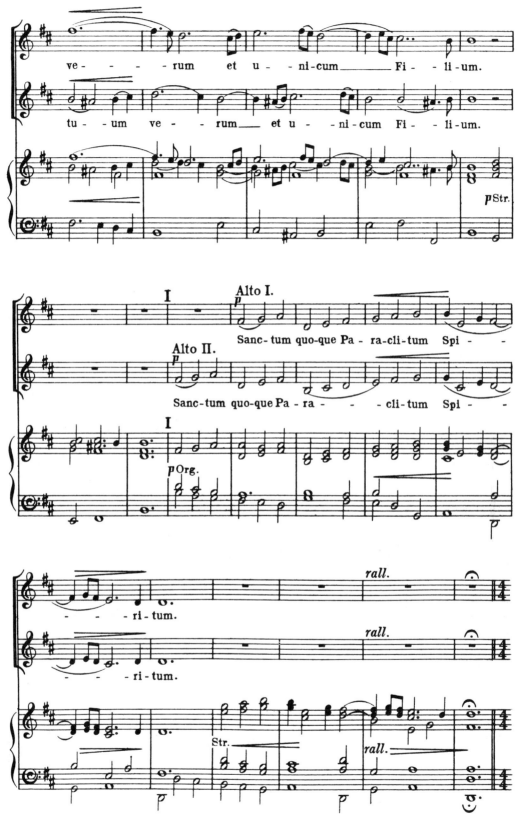

14

11415

* May be sung by a Soprano.

18

20

11415

Di-gna - re Do - mi-ne__ di - e__ i - - -

- sto si - - ne pec-ca - to nos cu-sto-di - - re

Do - mi - ne, Do-mi - ne mi-se-re-re, mi-se-

- re-re, mi-se - re-re no - stri Do - mi-ne mi - se - re - re,__

\* If this Solo is too high for a Male Alto, it might be sung by a Contralto or Soprano.